Suit Yourself

by
Mark Nicholls

This first edition published in Australia in 2019 by:

Prahran Publishing
P.O. Box 2041, Prahran, Victoria, 3181

© Copyright Mark Nicholls 2019

Mark Nicholls has asserted his legal and moral right under the Copyright Act 1968 to be identified as the author of this work.

Published by arrangement with
Prahran Publishing, Australia.

All rights are strictly reserved.

No part of this publication may be reproduced, stored in a retrieval system or transmitted, in any form or by any other means, without the publisher's prior permission in writing. Copying of this script for performance reasons is also strictly prohibited by law, either in whole or excerpts from.

This book is sold subject to the condition that it shall not, by way of trade or otherwise, be lent, resold, hired out or otherwise circulated without the publisher's prior consent in any form of binding or cover other than that in which it is published and without similar condition, including this condition, being imposed on the subsequent purchaser.

Every reasonable effort has been made to trace copyright holders of material reproduced in this book, but if any have been inadvertently overlooked the publishers would be glad to hear from them. The story, all names, characters, and incidents portrayed in this book are fictitious. No identification with actual persons past or present, places, buildings, and products is intended or should be inferred.

ISBN 978-1-922263-08-7 Paperback
ISBN 978-1-922263-09-4 eBook

Dewey: 822.4

A catalogue record for this book is available from the National Library of Australia

Performance Licensing and Royalty Payments

Mark Nicholls retains control of both the amateur and professional stage performance rights of this play. No unauthorised performance should occur without the express and written permission of the playwright.

Restriction of Alteration

There shall be no modifications of any kind to the play including deletion of dialogue (including objectionable language), changes to characters gender or names, title of the play or music without the express and written permission from the author.

Sound and Video Recordings

This play may contain stage directions to include the use of music, video or other sound recordings either in part or in whole. The author and the publisher have not sought the right to use such content and performance rights permission should be obtained seperately. Permission to record audio and video recordings of all performances must also be explicitly given by the author in writing.

Author Credit

Performance rights approval requires credit be given to Mark Nicholls as the sole and exclusive author of the play. This obligation applies to the title page of every program or other advertising material distributed in connection to this play. The author's credit should appear immediately under the title of the play on all published material, and alongside no other individual. Font size of credit cannot be less than 50% of the largest letter used in the play's title.

Please email info@prahran.press
for all performance enquiries.

Dedication

for Grace Taylor

About the Playwright

MARK NICHOLLS has been performing on various Melbourne stages since the age of six and has an extensive list of credits as a playwright, composer, singer, actor, producer and director. He is Senior Lecturer in Cinema Studies at the University of Melbourne where he has taught film since 1993.

He is the author of *Lost Objects of Desire: The Performances of Jeremy Irons* (2012), *Scorsese's Men: Melancholia and the Mob* (2004) and recently published articles on Italian Cinema, Powell and Pressburger's *The Red Shoes* and Sergei Diaghilev's celebrated company, The Ballets Russes.

Mark is a film critic and worked for many years on ABC Radio and for *The Age* newspaper, for which he wrote a weekly column between 2007 and 2009.

He lives in Melbourne with his partner, Ali Wirtz, and their two sons Oscar and Carlo.

Series Preface

I wrote these plays for only one reason, to perform them. I publish them here, therefore, somewhat reluctantly. They were never written to be read on the page by anyone but a treasured posy of performers that I trust to help me rescue them from it. They were certainly never conceived of as works of anything so respectable as literature. Nevertheless, I have found two reasons to overcome my reluctance and my usual roguish prejudice against readers and writers in favour of performers and punters. One reason is that putting these plays into print provides the opportunity for the most engaged of those who saw and heard them to revive and revise the experience. The other reason is archival. I wish to leave a permanent, if inadequate, record of the facts of their production over a decade, in a private space in Melbourne, for the benefit of both a small, dedicated paying audience, and for a smaller band of compulsive show-folk.

Writing these plays for the talented actors, musicians and backstage characters whose creations are recorded here, and having the privilege of working with these artists to produce them, has been the most satisfying occupation of my otherwise horrendously charmed and fascinating life.

Now that they have had their blessed release in print, these plays are beyond the concern of any motivation I had to write them. Read them, o curious one, and work it out for yourself! One motivation I will record, however, rests in the inspiration generously given by those who worked on and attended these cosy performances, and so brought their privileged, fleeting moments of theatre securely into being.

About the Play

Grace Taylor and Madeleine Swain sitting on a hillside and quietly discussing the problems of the world of their characters was a fascinating and enlightening theatrical experience. There is, however, an uncharacteristic and possibly sensational and distracting nastiness built into this play, as well as a certain degree of anger. Thankfully its contemplation of premeditated and strategic political violence is pure fantasy – at least as we currently understand it in the Australian context. Our knowledge of the facts of sexual abuse is not the thing that is commonplace. It's the sexual abuse (and the context in which it happens) that is commonplace. And we now know this and are less surprised by it.

Growing up in the 1970s, all the really spirited discussions in our family were about politics or church politics. The effect of this on me, I suspect, was that I have never really had any tolerance for the idea that the political is anything other than personal. If the God business can be riddled with self-interest, there can be no doubt that the business of state is equally narcissistic. I am perfectly willing to see this view as somewhat naïve, but when I hear genuinely outraged people saying things like, "hang on isn't he supposed to be a Christian?" or "wasn't she a trade unionist?", I feel vaguely alienated from the world and think I must be taking crazy pills. I suppose this is why I never really got past Freud and why melodrama remains my preferred genre. The problems of the familial and the domestic, let alone those of the unconscious, seem to me to be insoluble and, therefore, endlessly preoccupying.

CHARACTERS

JESSICA: a twenty-two-year-old journalism student.

BETH: fifty and The Leader of the Federal Parliamentary Opposition.

JEFF: forty-nine and The Federal Treasurer and Jessica's father.

PROLOGUE: to be played by actor playing Jeff.

The song in entre'act one and two is from Shakespeare's *As You Like It*.

Suit Yourself was first performed at Rear 4, Clifton Hill, Victoria on the 8th of November 2012 with the following cast:

Beth: Madeleine Swain

Jessica: Grace Taylor

Chorus/Jeff: Mark Nicholls

Director: Mark Nicholls

Co Producer: Alison Wirtz

Prologue:

JEFF (SINGS):

A mini-break is just as good as a holiday
You'll feel as if you've never been away
It's a great way to see places you want to visit
To see places that you'll never want to stay.
Hey!

I appreciate a healthy mobile signal
A roaming pleasure far from the banal
I'm partial to broad country communications
And good reception for my Radio Natzional
Snarl!

A mini-break is just as good as a holiday
You'll feel as if you've never been away
It's a great way to see places you want to visit
To see places that you'll never want to stay.
Hey!

I long for second-hand bookshops in the main street
A café run by local arty cliques
A place where city folk they like to gather
And poke around in search of cheap antiques
Eeek!

A mini-break is just as good as a holiday
You'll feel as if you've never been away
It's a great way to see places you want to visit
To see places that you'll never want to stay.
Hey!

I love the smell of country bacon in the morning
A cosy cottage all set up to please
A lazy glass of wine beneath the awning
(DVD, Blu-ray player, CD, AM/FM radio,
unlimited wireless internet access)
And ample tea and coffee making facilities
Please!

A mini-break is just as good as a holiday
You'll feel as if you've never been away
It's a great way to see places you want to visit
To see places that you'll never want to stay.

Act One
Scene One:

On a hill by the sea two Cape Cod style chairs face the audience. They stand on a grassy hill that eventually leads down to the sea. One chair is unoccupied. On the other sits JESSICA looking out to sea, but seeing nothing but the spectre of her own thoughts. Beside her on the grass are a folded newspaper, a notebook and pen and an iPhone. It is a fine, sunny morning. It is also Christmas Eve. In time BETH approaches from behind. She is carrying coffee things and the papers.

BETH: Hello! I didn't think anyone would be here.

JESSICA is in another world.

BETH gets nearer.

BETH: Hello! I said I didn't think anyone would be here.

JESSICA snaps out of her thoughts and turns around.

BETH: Oh. It's you. Jessica.

JESSICA: That's right. Beth! Sorry, I didn't expect anyone else to be here either.

BETH: I thought your grandparents were away.

JESSICA: They are. I just thought I'd break in and camp out here for a few days. You know, the whole Christmas thing.

BETH: I do. I'm doing the same sort of thing.

JESSICA: You don't have a family, do you?

BETH: I've got what you've got, pretty much. But only just. Add twenty years and some nursing home action.

JESSICA: No, I mean no husband and kids.

BETH: No. *[She sits down.]* So, you are not doing Christmas with Jeff?

JESSICA: I never do Christmas with Jeff, or anything much else for that matter. I'm not going to start anything this year I might not want to keep up.

BETH: No friends to go to?

JESSICA: I did get a couple of offers, but they made it sound like I was doing them a favour.

BETH: What the welcome stranger keeping families from each other's throats routine?

JESSICA: Yeah something like that. Not very appealing.

BETH: I can see that.

Act I – Scene 1

JESSICA: Anyway, I've got work to do. Actually, you might be able to help me. You know all this low-level terrorist stuff going on? *The Age* said if I had anything good they might publish a feature.

BETH: If you're talking about what Fred called those "three completely unrelated episodes of urban vandalism" last month, I would hardly call it terrorism."

JEESSICA: Fred?

BETH: The Attorney General.

JESSICA: What, so a Molotov cocktail chucked at the Environment Minister is not terrorism?

BETH: Chucked at the Environment Minister's chicken shed, actually. And a bit of graffiti on the odd electoral office hardly counts as conspiracy. *[Pause]* You know once, when your grandfather was Prime Minister, someone spray-painted his fence with the charming phrase "Rich cunts".

JESSICA: What did he do?

BETH: Nothing very much. He just said, "That's not fair. We're not rich." Anyway since when did you become an *Age* journalist?

JESSICA: I'm not. I'm doing second year journalism at RMIT and I just pitched them the idea.

BETH: Do they know who you are?

JESSICA: So, you don't think I could get the gig on my own?

BETH: How should I know? I just know how newspapers work. If the Treasurer's daughter wants to write a story about anti-government vandalism they are hardly going to say no.

JESSICA: I use my mother's name, actually.

BETH: Oh, that's right. If a former Prime Minister's granddaughter wants to write a story about anti-government vandalism they are hardly going to say no!

JESSICA: Kinda caught, aren't I?

BETH: Kind of. Anyway, it doesn't look like it's going to happen. I don't see much evidence of activity in that notebook.

JESSICA: Well, that is where you can help. Can you give me a few quotable quotes?

BETH: Are you mad? Then it certainly won't get published. The Treasurer's daughter, or a Prime Minister's granddaughter, filing a story may be news, but the Opposition Leader's next-door neighbour filing a story is definitely not news.

JESSICA: It would be if we were having an affair?

BETH: Would you go that far just to get your story in the paper?

Act I – Scene 1

JESSICA: I was thinking it would get me in with your press guy. He's pretty cute!

BETH: He would welcome the opportunity to get me into the papers. But if I have to get screwed to do it, he usually prefers to arrange it himself.

JESSICA: He's not gay?

BETH: No he's not. But he is a pimp. Anyway, from what I understand, you shouldn't have any trouble getting in there. I'll introduce you.

JESSICA: Jeff tried to pimp me last night at that bloody Christmas ball.

BETH: Oh yes?

JESSICA: He tried to push two 'B and S' types on me. He said these boys were 'with the party' and wouldn't it be fantastic if I had a drink with them?

BETH: Oh God, what did you do?

JESSICA: Nothing, I just said 'no thanks' and that 'this party would be much better if there were a few more boys here who were against it'.

BETH: That would have confused him.

JESSICA: He didn't really get it.

BETH: Last night was a bit like that wasn't it?

JESSICA: It's always like that. Don't you ever think when you're at one of those stupid parties, 'What the hell am I doing here?' Melbourne and Sydney ex-private school political class constantly reconvening on the flimsiest pretexts in order to celebrate the survival of the status quo.

BETH: Good line.

JESSICA: I thought so. In fact I have been rehearsing it all morning.

They pause to look at the ocean.

BETH: We've never really talked, have we? I mean considering I have lived next door to your grandparents for twenty years.

JESSICA: I didn't think you liked me very much.

BETH: Why?

JESSICA: Most people your age, especially without kids, usually find kids pretty annoying.

BETH: Do they? Perhaps you were annoying. Anyway, that doesn't explain what you are doing here now.

JESSICA: I didn't come to visit you. I didn't even know you would be here. Anyway, why should there be any mystery about me being here. I told you why.

Act I – Scene 1

BETH: No one likes to wake up to an empty house on Christmas morning, if they have the option. I think even I'd go to Jeff's if he asked me.

JESSICA: I'd love to see you and Jeff around the tree opening prezzies in your nighties and jimjams.

BETH: I don't wear one.

JESSICA: Even better still.

BETH: So what's going on?

JESSICA: Nothing. Well, if you must know, I'm nursing a broken heart.

BETH: Ah, got dumped did you?

JESSICA: Not exactly. I just don't think it's ever going to get off the ground. He's kind of keen but he's got a woman hanging around.

BETH: Great. On the verge but not quite in. That's the best part. Go on, tell me the story.

JESSICA: There's no story. We have been hanging around together and we had a bit of a kiss, but then he told me about the other one. So I think that even if it does happen, he's probably totally dodgy and he'd probably do it all over again to me when I'm in her place, so what's the point?

BETH: People change. Anyway, surely there's no one quite like Jessica?

JESSICA: That's what I think, but the idea doesn't seem to be taking shape, at least in his mind. So I'm down here wallowing in grief and proving my love to all the world by shunning society – at least until New Year's.

BETH: It's also the first Christmas since your mother died.

JESSICA: Yep.

BETH: How do you feel about it?

JESSICA: It doesn't really feel much different to any other time. In fact, it's all a bit of a relief. I thought it would be horrible.

BETH: Everyone else always makes such a fuss about it.

JESSICA: God, I wish they wouldn't. Jeff is the worst. Ten months later and people are just starting to forget about you as the dead woman's daughter and then you cop another round of taboo recognition, just because it's Christmas.

BETH: He's giving you a hard time, is he?

JESSICA: He's always giving me a hard time. Nothing I ever do is right. Everything he wants me to do seems totally off the planet. Why do people have kids if they just expect them to act like Mini Me all the time?

BETH: Perhaps he's not coping.

Act I – Scene 1

JESSICA: He dumped her. And that was fifteen years ago. It's a bit rich if he's going to start harassing me because he feels guilty now.

BETH: But you said he's always been like that?

JESSICA: We've never got on. He doesn't understand me at all. He thinks I'm some sort of lesbo-lefty-feminist and he can't seem to get over it. I suppose he just associates me with Mum and lumps us into the same category, but I'm not really like her at all.

BETH: First I have heard about Alice being gay.

JESSICA: I mean in the lefty-feminist way.

BETH: Ah, yet another factional division! That lot are splitting like healthy stock in a recession.

JESSICA: I don't think he ever really understood her anyway, so there was no chance for me. You may as well give up. He's so obsessed with the idea that Alice and I are the enemy (were the enemy) that we are virtually doing your job for you. *[She pauses.]* It's odd, Jeff is probably the most hated person in the country but all that stuff doesn't really mean anything to me. I love politics, but I am not at all interested in policy. I admit it. Politics is just the family business. I don't give a rat's about taxation or working families or carbon emissions. I don't judge him for any of that rubbish. Besides, plenty of people's parents do things that other people don't like. When you think about it, how many lawyers or businessmen or even doctors and community workers can ever really say that what they're doing is for anyone other than themselves? I don't expect Jeff to be a philanthropist. I just wish he would give me a break and take the same line with me.

BETH: It's a bit hard for him to show some genuine empathy for you if you keep running away.

JESSICA: What do you mean?

BETH: There's nothing like a Christmas reconciliation. Besides, if you give it a go with Jeff you might find it's a bit easier now.

JESSICA: Why? Because it's Christmas?

BETH: No, I mean since your mum died.

JESSICA: How?

BETH: Well, I don't really think Jeff would give a damn if he thought you were some raging International Socialist. In fact, he'd probably love it. But I can see how you might think that he sees you in those terms. Actually, he's a lot like you. Perhaps we all are. It's not just a *West Wing* cliché. Politics really does come before policy. And personalities come before politics. If he treats you like he imagines you have dreadlocks and sell the Green Left Weekly outside Flinders Street, it's just that he feels distanced from you. The only way he can really interact with you in those circumstances is to conjure up a category to fit you in. What is between you is a lot smaller than that and, in some ways, a lot bigger and he knows it.

JESSICA: But what has that got to do with Alice?

BETH: Perhaps Alice was the thing between you? Now that she's gone, you both have to face up to the fact that you have no one to fight over.

JESSICA: I doubt he ever felt that strongly about her.

BETH: No, he did. Believe me. *[Looking off.]* Anyway, you can ask him yourself.

JESSICA: What do you mean?

BETH: Well, unless your grandfather has come back from his holiday, and he has finally started using a Commonwealth car, that must be Jeff coming up the driveway.

JESSICA: That's weird. God, I can't even escape for two days. Can't he even take a break at Christmas? That poor com. car driver is probably dying to get home and Jeff's got him out here.

BETH: You underestimate your dad's capacity for charm. They love him in the drivers department. This guy will probably be still delivering presents for him at lunchtime tomorrow.

JEFF enters.

JESSICA: *[To JEFF]* Hi. What's going on?

JEFF: I didn't know you were here. I thought you were with Gran.

JESSICA: Only in spirit.

JEFF: Do you want to come and have Christmas dinner with us? Margaret's got plenty of food.

JESSICA: No, I am having a Scrooge Christmas. Ask Beth why. She knows all the details. Anyway, what are you doing here?

JEFF: There's some stuff happening. I just wanted to speak to Beth about it.

JESSICA: What's happening?

JEFF: I can't say. *[To BETH]* There's a story breaking tonight about the thing and I need to ask you to hold off from commenting, at least until after Christmas?

BETH: *[Getting interested]* What is it I am supposed to comment on?

JESSICA: Not to comment on, Beth.

BETH: Well, whatever.

JEFF: It's that refugee thing actually. I don't want a huge thing in the press right now. So if you could at least show me that courtesy.

JESSICA: Good try, Dad. But you really came down to take me back to Melbourne, didn't you?

Act I – Scene 1

JEFF: *[Suppressed smile]* When did you get so politically savvy?

JESSICA: I had good teachers.

BETH: I was actually feeling quite important for a second there. *[Getting up]* Bye, Jeff, as this is clearly going to be a father-daughter moment, for which I have neither the experience nor the inclination, I'll go and get lunch. Unless, of course, you are going to stay? I have decided that I am staying right here on this hill for at least the next twenty-four hours and I advise you, Jessica, to stay too. We can alternate getting picnic supplies.

JESSICA: I'm in.

BETH: Good. What about you Jeff?

JEFF: Thanks all the same. I am not really dressed for picnicking.

BETH: Pity. Anyway, Happy Christmas Jeff. *[She moves off.]*

JEFF: Yeah. Merry Christmas. *[To JESSICA]* I've forgotten how cocky she can be. She's rubbish in the House, but outside she can be a real smartarse.

JESSICA: You think she should save her wit for Parliament, Dad?

JEFF: That's what she's paid for. She's just not very good at public confrontation.

JESSICA: A back room girl you think?

JEFF: Yeah. Subtle. So why are you spending time with her?

JESSICA: Perhaps that is the way she operates?

JEFF: Nice try.

JESSICA: I just bumped into her here. In fact, I hardly know her at all. When did she move here? I don't remember her being about at all when we were kids?

JEFF: I think it was after your grandfather retired.

JESSICA: Did they know each other before that?

JEFF: Yeah. In fact I think Beth knew your grandparents before I did.

JESSICA: Did she know Mum?

JEFF: Of course. We all knew each other at uni. We used to hang out together.

JESSICA: God, what happened?

JEFF: What do you mean?

JESSICA: I can't imagine you lot 'hanging out' at all.

JEFF: You'd be surprised. In fact, Beth and I were pretty much best friends in those days. We used to hang out a lot. Lots of hanging out and lots of drinking.

Act I – Scene 1

JESSICA: So what did happen. You are so different!

JEFF: We're not so different. Anyway, life happens. People move on, situations change. It's hard to keep up.

JESSICA: Working together in the same building should help.

JEFF: You would think so. But I know two blokes who work in the city. They were inseparable friends at school and uni for about 12 years, then they drifted apart. Twenty years later they found out that they had been working in the same building ever since.

JESSICA: Did they get back together?

JEFF: They tried it, but they found out they couldn't stand each other. Adults aren't very good at friendships.

JESSICA: Why not?

JEFF: With men it's probably something to do with sex.

JESSICA: What, do you mean women?

JEFF: No. It's probably something to do with our mothers.

JESSICA: And now none of us has got one.

JEFF: What do you mean?

JESSICA:	You, me and Beth. Three poor motherless creatures!
JEFF:	All the more reason for you to come back to town.
JESSICA:	You just don't want me off the leash when the press get onto your refugee thing. God, do you really think that I'd get involved in that one? I am not great with the press, but I know enough to keep my mouth shut.
JEFF:	Except that you are writing a story for *The Age*!
JESSICA:	Of course! So you know about that. Yeah, well it's on the violence against polis thing, not on refugees. You should thank me. It's your gang that's getting beaten up! And besides, for someone with my family background you don't give me much credit.
JEFF:	I knew your mother.
JESSICA:	That's an awful thing to say. She never did any harm to your career.
JEFF:	You think that, do you?
JESSICA:	Well, I'm not coming. Don't worry. If Channel Nine come calling I'll keep out of sight.
JEFF:	You might consider being in sight when they come to me about it!
JESSICA:	Why, are you after the rainbow vote now, Dad?

Act I – Scene 1

JEFF: What? Oh, so now you're gay! Seriously, can't you give me a bit of support, now and then? You'll benefit in the end.

JESSICA: Yeah right. "So in accepting this Walkley Award for excellence in print journalism, I just want to thank my father for all the support he gave me by arsing around in party politics for thirty years, achieving virtually nothing for the country and teaching me the real meaning of quality family time." That's a joke.

JEFF: I suppose so. *[He pauses to take it in and then stands up.]* I'll put your Christmas money on the credit card.

JESSICA: Thanks.

JEFF: See ya.

JESSICA: Bye.

JEFF: *[Sincerely if somewhat rehearsed.]* I'm sorry it's like that. Perhaps when you have children you will realise how easy it is to make little mistakes, and how things can really stuff up on the back of those little mistakes. Anyway, I'm doing what I can.

JEFF leaves and Jessica is left standing.

End scene.

Entr'acte:

JESSICA (SINGS):

Blow, Blow, thou winter wind
Blow, Blow, thou winter wind
Thou art not so unkind
As man's ingratitude
As man's ingratitude.

Blow, Blow, thou winter wind
Blow, Blow, thou winter wind
Thy tooth is not so keen
Because thou art not seen
Although thy breath be rude

Sing hey-ho, sing hey-ho, unto the green holly
Most friendship mere feigning, most loving, mere folly
This life is most jolly.

End Entr'acte.

Act One
Scene Two:

The scene is as before, except a table of food and wine has been added to the scene. It is lunchtime and BETH and JESSICA are chatting and picking at food and wine.

JESSICA: I'm sorry about that thing this morning with Dad.

BETH: Don't be. I'm used to it. In fact I think I probably contributed to it.

JESSICA: In what sense?

BETH: I aggravate your father.

JESSICA: That's your job, isn't it?

BETH: Yes. But that's not what I mean.

JESSICA: What do you mean?

BETH: I am talking about the past.

JESSICA: I have just been hearing about all that hanging out and drinking business.

BETH: I thought you might one day.

JESSICA: It's just so hard to believe. You seem so different.

BETH: We weren't then. We're not now. Not really. Career politicians are quite similar basically – whichever side you're on. We all want the same things and think in the same policy terms. It's mainly about the detail.

JESSICA: So what was the detail?

BETH: In our case it was a quarrel. The kind of quarrel that never really comes out and so it never gets cleared up and ends up being deferred onto other things.

JESSICA: Like federal politics?

BETH: Not exactly. But similar things.

JESSICA: So, what was it all about?

BETH: Your mother actually.

JESSICA: Alice?

BETH: Yeah. At least she was the bone of contention.

JESSICA: What happened?

BETH: The whole thing was madness. I had just come out of a long relationship, pretty worse for wear. *[Pause]* Actually it was with Jeff.

JESSICA: My God!

BETH: Yes. The three of us were all very close, but somehow Jeff and I managed to break away and we had been together, secretly, for quite a while. Then one day he just suddenly broke it off. No explanation at all. I was really upset and so, finally, I told Alice the whole story. I had to. Apart from Jeff, I didn't have anyone else I could talk to about that kind of thing. Anyway, she was very kind to me about it – probably too kind – and so, very quickly, I became overly dependent on her. Then she went to England with your grandmother – probably to get away from me – and, like an idiot, I followed her. When I arrived in London she met me off the plane and was perfectly sweet to me. You see, I had a pretty strong sense about her ambivalence over our friendship and on the flight over I got really drunk on the free booze and tortured myself that she was going to fob me off as soon as I arrived. She didn't, of course, and we spent three perfect days together in a friend's flat, just hanging out and talking. It was bliss. I didn't blink when she told me she was going to the country for the weekend and didn't ask me to come. Later that night I was having dinner with an old friend – I remember it was perfect twilight evening – and she phoned me from the station and told me that she loved me – a somewhat unexpected announcement! Three days later, as we had planned, I arrived in Cornwall, and Alice was out, so I spent the afternoon in the garden – chatting with your grandmother, actually. Then about eight, we were having a drink before a kind of a dinner party, lots of people about, and suddenly Alice just waltzed in arm in arm with Jeff. I didn't even know he was in the country.

JESSICA: What?

BETH: They had been together the whole time. Or at least since just before he dumped me.

JESSICA: Hell. What did you do?

BETH: I don't really remember. I think your grandmother saw what was going on and took me off to the other end of the party, as if nothing had happened. I must have spent the entire evening in a sort of a daze. Next morning I woke up feeling absolutely clear about the whole thing, and unusually energetic. So I just got up, caught the train back to London, walked back to the flat in the rain and spent the next two hours sitting on the bed sobbing.

JESSICA: It must have been horrible!

BETH: It was for a while. But I got over it.

JESSICA: Did you ever forgive them?

BETH: Yes, eventually. I was certainly pretty pissed off with them, especially with Jeff actually, which was probably unfair. Or perhaps I was just shocked and disappointed. It's hard to blame someone for falling in love. It was more the way he handled the situation. I think I felt that both of them were guilty of weakness and a certain amount of deception. I put Alice under a lot of pressure. I was very needy. She had every right to walk away from it. But Jeff couldn't really cope and he responded really badly. He'd never really done a shitty thing in his life. In the scheme of things, going off with Alice wasn't particularly shitty. It's just

Act I – Scene 2

                that instead of attempting some sort of token apology or excuse, he went the other way and dug in defensively.

JESSICA: I am not sure I understand if you were in love with Jeff or with Alice, or both?

BETH: Probably both.

JESSICA: So what did you do?

BETH: After I left them in England and came home I hardly saw them for months. Then one night Alice just turned up at my place in floods of tears. They had had a huge fight and I think she was seeing a side to Jeff that neither of us had ever seen. It's funny how when you are in your twenties you think you know your best friends, but you don't really. Anyway, she stayed with me in my flat for a little while until it all calmed down and then, one day, she went back to Jeff. In fact that was about the time when she became pregnant with you.

JESSICA: So Jeff tried to blame you for that one too?

BETH: Sort of. But don't worry. I'm not your father. But that was about the point when he came down pretty hard on me though.

JESSICA: He must have been out of his mind.

BETH: He was. Although he had some encouragement from Alice.

JESSICA: What do you mean?

BETH: When she went back to him, Jeff started going off about me and he became obsessed with what Alice and I were up to, and talking about, all that time. When she saw his reaction to the situation, she just refused to discuss it with him. That, of course, infuriated Jeff.

JESSICA: Which is what she wanted.

BETH: Probably. Not really. Although I sometimes like to think that she wanted it to be true.

JESSICA: What?

BETH: What Jeff was so worried about! You know, girl talk. The expression of feelings, emotions and mutual support, all leading to a state of intimacy specifically designed to exclude men – or at least designed to exclude Jeff.

JESSICA: Do you think she was in love with you?

BETH: I doubt it. She respected me, but I doubt she had any real feelings of love for me. No more than I ever had for her. In a funny way I think she was in love with the idea of the three of us.

JESSICA: This is getting interesting.

BETH: Not as interesting as all that. No, I mean, the relationship between the three of us was what was important to her. We were very close in those years. I think she was probably shocked when she realised that Jeff and I had peeled off. That was probably pretty disturbing for her and so the only way she could help from feeling left out of it all was to do the same

Act I – Scene 2

thing. Then when she saw what Jeff could be like and how hurt and upset I was over the break-up, she grew closer to me. You see what she was doing? It was all about trying to bring us all together and smooth over the hurt. A state of intimacy specifically designed to exclude no one.

JESSICA: Come on. You can tell me if there was any girl on girl stuff with you guys.

BETH: What is it about your generation? As far as I understand it from the Sunday papers, you straight girls just seem to use 'girl on girl', as you call it, simply as a way of impressing timid and nervous boys.

JESSICA: There's something in that. And it never really works anyway.

BETH: Of course not! Those poor boys don't want you; they just want to be you.

JESSICA: So why do you think she married him?

BETH: You really don't like Jeff, do you? *[She says nothing.]* I wish you could think of him as I knew him. We had great times together. Alice was particularly romantic and nostalgic about that period. It was important to her. But I don't think she would have married him but for you. I hope you don't mind me saying that?

JESSICA: So, it's all really my fault?

BETH: I wouldn't say that. I'd just say that you were the result of it all.

JESSICA: Yeah well I wish I wasn't.

BETH: Oh come on. The wounded politician's daughter bit can only get you so far, surely! With your family background, I would have thought you might have developed a few coping strategies by now. Talk to your grandmother.

JESSICA: He's just such an utter bastard.

BETH: Well, he's hardly the first leonine alpha male to have difficulty relating to his children. His approach may be a little awkward, but at least he tries. I've just seen him.

JESSICA: He's been trying all my life. Awkward is not the word, more like perverse.

BETH: That's a bit harsh.

JESSICA: You think!

BETH: What are we talking about?

JESSICA: You know it's just very interesting to hear about all this Dutch-door stuff between you three.

BETH: What? I told you, it wasn't really like that.

JESSICA: Sorry, that's very hard to believe.

BETH: It's true.

Act I – Scene 2

JESSICA: What in Bill Clinton land? "I didn't actually stick my dick in her, she just sucked me off a little bit, so we didn't actually have sex, Your Honour."

BETH: That's not what it was at all.

JESSICA: No? You had him, then she had him and then to smooth it all over, she had you.

BETH: You are missing the point.

JESSICA: Well, I am not, actually. In fact, I think I have a pretty good idea about it all.

BETH: Why are you so upset about this? What are we talking about?

JESSICA: Well, let's just say it's pretty easy for me to see the whole thing in terms of a certain lax attitude towards boundaries.

BETH: What?

JESSICA looks at BETH and says nothing.

JESSICA: *[Finally]* Let's just say I know a lot about fathers and their awkwardness of approach when it comes to relating to their children.

BETH: *[Taking it in]* What exactly do you mean?

JESSICA: I don't want to go into the details.

BETH: *[Can hardly think how to respond.]* All right. *[Pause]* But you are telling me that...

JESSICA: Yes. Happy Christmas!

Pause.

BETH: *[Still faltering]* So what happ... *[Can't finish that question.]* Did he... *[Nor that one]*. You mean he raped you?

Pause.

JESSICA: I don't know. I don't call it that. You're the legislator, what would you call it?

BETH: When did it happen?

JESSICA: Right, so timing is everything. Oh, it went on.

BETH: How old were you?

JESSICA: Old enough to know what I was doing, and what he was doing. Just apparently not old enough to know how much it was going to fuck me up. And fuck him up apparently. It's a bit like teenage drinking, or, even better still, children under twelve not crossing at the lights. Until you are a certain age you can't really see how fast the car is going to come and knock the shit out of you. So I don't exactly see it as rape because part of me knew exactly what was going on, and another tiny, infantile and socially awkward part of me also knew what was going on and saw no reason to stop it. You can't really stop a ten-year-old from at least wanting to cross a hundred metres before the level crossing.

Act I – Scene 2 31

BETH: You were ten?

JESSICA: I suppose it started about the time he split up with Alice and then stopped when Margaret came on the scene. You can see why I have always been fond of Margaret, in spite of that stubborn little moustache she has that seems to defy all reasonable attempts at bleaching.

BETH: Did you ever tell Alice? Or anyone else for that matter?

JESSICA: Of course not!

BETH: I suppose it was too hard.

JESSICA: No skin off my nose. You don't tell anyone because you feel ashamed for the sicko, when you realise that is what he is, or was. You also don't tell anyone because no one will understand it at all. No one could really let themselves believe it. It's too disturbing. To be honest, the one person I didn't want to disturb was Mum. I thought about it. You know I actually contemplated telling her when she was dying. I couldn't do it. If anyone had a reason to see Dad's capacity for something like that it was her. But I just couldn't put that into the mix. I don't know who I was protecting. I just couldn't do it.

BETH: What about Jeff?

JESSICA: I think you have to be able to look someone in the eye to do that. After a romance like ours, that is somewhat impossible.

BETH: Romance?

JESSICA: That's what it is you know.

BETH: You think?

JESSICA: Oh Beth. I thought you were a hard-headed politician and it seems you have fallen for the greatest myth of all. Romance isn't all Valentine's Day and 'I WUV U' balloons, trips to Paris and *When Harry Met Sally*. It's all about pain and suffering. An old witch, not played by Meg Ryan, shows you a vision of your future and it's filled with passion and intensity and awesome sex. Then she says to you that to have it you are going to spend the rest of eternity burning in Hell. So what do you do?

BETH: You go for it.

JESSICA: Yep. Bring it on. Like a real idiot.

Pause.

BETH: Do you think he thinks about it? Has he ever said anything?

JESSICA: Of course not! I doubt he thinks about it. How could you, and go on?

BETH: Do you suffer from it?

JESSICA: No. My experience was pretty tame, from what I hear. I don't suffer. I just have been blessed with an overdose of irony. And cursed.

Act I – Scene 2

[She gets up.] Anyway, to celebrate, let's get a bottle of Prosecco. I feel strangely exhilarated. Sorry. It's a lot to put on you at Christmas without some sparkling wine.

JESSICA moves off to get the wine. BETH is astounded and exhausted. After a while she reaches for her phone and makes a call.

End scene.

Entr'acte:

BETH (SINGS):

Freeze, freeze, thou bitter sky,
Freeze, freeze, thou bitter sky,
That dost not bite so night
As benefits forgot,
As benefits forgot.

Freeze, freeze, thou bitter sky,
Freeze, freeze, thou bitter sky,
Al(though) thou the waters warp,
Thy sting is not so sharp,
As friends remembered not.

Sing hey-ho, sing hey-ho, unto the green holly
Most friendship mere feigning, most loving, mere folly
This life is most jolly.

End Entre'Acte

Act One
Scene Three:

The scene is as before. It is early evening. JESSICA and BETH are sitting nearly through the bottle of Prosecco mentioned at the end of the previous scene. BETH's phone rings and she takes the call and wanders off as she does, then returns.

JESSICA: What was that?

BETH: It's Jeff. He's been attacked outside the house in Malvern.

JESSICA: Attacked? What do you mean?

BETH: Apparently some guys in a car stopped him as he was driving into the house. That was the office. They said he's fine, some people driving by stopped and frightened them away and then they took Jeff to the Alfred.

JESSICA: Who or what are they? He only left a short while ago. What happened exactly?

BETH: He's been attacked by someone outside the house.

JESSICA: What do you mean?

BETH: He's all right. He's just been frightened and a bit knocked about.

JESSICA: How far did they get?

BETH: Far enough to put him into hospital for the night. They say he's OK, but he's pretty badly beaten up.

JESSICA: Who were they?

BETH: I've no idea.

JESSICA: So a carful of goons just turned up outside his house on Christmas Eve and laid into him? They must have planned it. What on Earth is going on?

BETH: It's OK Jessica. He's fine. I'm sure it sounds much worse than it is. It was probably just some local kids trying it on.

JESSICA: Kids? That's fairly unlikely isn't it.

BETH: Well, you know. This isn't the US. He hardly has a massive secret service detail with him twenty-four seven. It has been done before.

Pause.

JESSICA: *[Lost in thoughts of their previous conversation.]* So why didn't you just have him beaten up here?

BETH: What are you talking about?

JESSICA: They were your guys, weren't they?

BETH: My guys? *[Long pause.]* Perhaps they were.

Act I – Scene 2

JESSICA: *[Snapping out of it.]* Now you're joking

BETH: You asked the question.

JESSICA: Yes, but I didn't expect that answer.

BETH: What made you think of it that way?

JESSICA: Hang on. So now you're telling me...

BETH: Yes Jessica, let's say I am telling you.

JESSICA: And the others too?

BETH: Which others?

JESSICA: The farm thing and the electorate office and the other stuff. You know *The Age* story?

BETH: No. Nothing to do with me. You're stuck on the other things because you think they helped you work this one out. But they're totally unrelated. Well, not totally unrelated – in the sense that they are part of the same problem.

JESSICA: Meaning?

BETH: People are pissed off, Jessica. The low-level terrorist thing you have been looking at is being beaten up by the government because they think it might get them some sympathy. All the other things were done by totally unrelated people. It had to come. Look, government in this country is so distant from people's lives and so out of touch that they are doing things and they don't have the slightest idea of the consequences. They just don't know what's going on out there. All you have to do is look at their security arrangements to see how out of touch they are. Well, think of what happened to Jeff tonight. God, forget One Nation or the bloody bikie gangs. It was inevitable some people might turn towards a vague form of violence, even just to try to elicit some measure of empathy.

JESSICA: Is that what you want?

BETH: Not personally, but others do.

JESSICA: So you thought you'd have Jeff beaten up so that others would feel better?

BETH: No, that's not it at all.

JESSICA: So why did you do it?

BETH: How good a journalist are you, Jessica?

JESSICA: To be honest, I'm faltering a little. I can't quite believe we're having this conversation.

BETH: I'm glad.

JESSICA: Why?

BETH: For one thing it shows that what you think I have done is almost totally unbelievable. For another it means that as a journalist you are not totally desensitised.

JESSICA: I don't think I really want to be that good.

Act I – Scene 2

BETH: Come on Jess, this is an interview. Give me the right answer and there's a job in it for you in the PM's office, if I ever get there.

JESSICA: Is that a bribe?

BETH: I don't need to bribe you. You won't go after this story because no on would believe you. The lawyers at *The Age* won't let you print because there's no evidence. It's just too untidy, especially if you put it with the other stuff. The longer you try to chase this the weirder you'll look – you'll wreck your career.

JESSICA: You're taking a big risk telling me, anyway. What if I decide it's too important and go after it anyway.

BETH: It's unlikely that you would. And I want to ask you – with your, what shall I say, perspective – if you should reveal this story or if it might be better to let it go.

JESSICA: Why on earth would I condone political terrorism?

BETH: It's hardly that.

JESSICA: I think it is.

BETH: Say it is. Why did we do it?

JESSICA: Why did you do it? You wanted to scare the shit out of Jeff and put him out of action for a while.

BETH: That's right. But it might have the opposite effect. It might actually have the effect that the government is hoping for with the terrorism beat-up and make Jeff dig in. Look at the mileage the Liberals got out of the panic over seventy-five. Panic and terror are good for conservatives.

JESSICA: That's unlikely, but even if he does dig in, it'd be a major distraction for the government. It would risk placing him in the centre of the action, which is not where they want him, given that he's so unpopular.

BETH: But it's still a risk.

JESSICA: Yes. So what's it all about?

BETH: Empathy I suppose. You see, people like Jeff have no idea what it is to suffer. They are so cut off from ordinary people by money and power, that they have no idea of the consequences of their actions.

JESSICA: So putting Jeff in hospital for the night is going to achieve that?

BETH: Not necessarily. But it might provide a bit of personal insecurity that will make it interesting for him. You see, unlike you, he's never known the horrible feeling when you lose a job, or when your son gets kidnapped in Cambodia and foreign affairs are doing nothing because they don't want to offend a foreign government. Or what it's like to have your husband killed in Balibo and have nothing done about it because the government

Act I – Scene 2

doesn't want to offend the Indonesians. But if he's never known that, he now knows what it's like to be scared, defenseless and utterly lacking in control – which many of the rest of the country know, partly due to him, every day.

JESSICA: You've known him all these years – how do you think he'll react?

BETH: It's hard to say. He's quite a tragic figure, Jeff. It could push him over the edge all together.

JESSICA: And give you government?

BETH: It's possible.

JESSICA: It's callous to be sitting here talking so casually about the fact that you have just paid a bunch of thugs to beat someone up.

BETH: Yes, it is. But it's no more callous than some of the conversations that go on in Cabinet, which are far more pervasive in their effect. Think of the effect on the environment as a result of the cabinet discussion on Kyoto? What about the effect on Philip Barnes's parents when the government decided to do nothing for him when he was kidnapped in Cambodia? What you think I've done is reprehensible, but perhaps also justified.

JESSICA: What gives you the right to say that? If you do get into government how will you be any different?

BETH: If I thought we wouldn't be any different I wouldn't bother.

JESSICA: I thought it was all about the detail? If you are too different you'll get booted out after a term, so what's the point?

BETH: You know the system. Legislation very rarely gets rolled back – the politics are too difficult.

JESSICA: I'm feeling slightly nauseated.

BETH: I'm sorry – it's a lot to let you in on. A lot of responsibility.

JESSICA: Responsibility?

BETH: You now have to decide how to act morally, given what you know. I don't envy you.

JESSICA: What would you do in my place?

BETH: I don't know. I'm glad I don't have to think about it.

JESSICA: So why did you risk telling me all this? If you don't know how I'll act?

BETH: I'm like you were earlier this evening. I just had to tell someone. You are the lucky one. Happy Christmas! You're the keeper of the mystery. Now that you know my horrible story we are yoked together. You can ring me from time to time – to keep me on track. See if I am going to blow my cover. Or yours for that matter.

Act I – Scene 2

JESSICA: So you think your secret is like mine?

BETH: I think Freud calls them "the two basic laws of totemism", don't have sex with the totem and don't kill it.

JESSICA: But you didn't kill Jeff.

BETH: You can't do harm to it either.

JESSICA: So Jeff is taboo?

BETH: Just now he is. But these things don't last long. Sooner or later they are done away with.

JESSICA: Then what happens?

BETH: No one cares any more. Taboo goes back to the rubbish.

JESSICA: You have changed your tune about Jeff. This afternoon it was all about understanding and forgiveness.

BETH: I wasn't talking like a politician then. Oh and then it became all about rape.

Pause.

JESSICA: You didn't have anything to do with this hospital job did you?

BETH: Of course not. I didn't have anything to do with four guys ramming their car into Jeff's car, smashing the bonnet and the windows with lead pipes, and then pulling Jeff out of the car and going over him in much the same way. No. I didn't have anything to do with that.

JESSICA: So why did you let me think you did?

BETH: Because I wish I had. In fact, I think I owe it to him.

Curtain.

www.ingramcontent.com/pod-product-compliance
Lightning Source LLC
Chambersburg PA
CBHW071320080526
44587CB00018B/3302